D1143117

First published 2014 by Macmillan Children's Books
a division of Macmillan Publishers Limited
20 New Wharf Road, London N1 9RR
Basingstoke and Oxford
Associated companies throughout the world
www.panmacmillan.com

ISBN 978-1-4472-7815-3

Text copyright © Macmillan Children's Books 2014
Photography © Getty images with the following exception:
FOX Image Collection via Getty Images p38.

9 8 7 6 5 4 3 2 1

A CIP catalogue record for this book is available from
the British Library.

Written by Emily Stead
Designed by Claire Yeo

Printed in China

NIALL
IN MY POCKET

NIALL HORAN

BORN: 13 SEPTEMBER 1993

BIRTHPLACE:
MULLINGAR, IRELAND

HEIGHT: 1 M 71 CM

'USE YOUR **SMILE** TO CHANGE THE WORLD.'

LIKE HIS BANDMATE LIAM, NIALL'S STAR SIGN IS

VIRGO.

VIRGOS ARE SAID TO BE INDEPENDENT AND HELPFUL.

NIALL'S FIRST SNOG WAS WITH A FRENCH EXCHANGE STUDENT.

OOH-LA-LA!

APART FROM ON STAGE, NIALL'S FAVOURITE PLACE TO SING IS IN THE SHOWER!

WHEN
NIALL GETS
FLUSTERED,
HIS FAVOURITE
PHRASE IS,
**'CHEESEBURGERS
AND JELLY BABIES!'**

NIALL OFTEN TALKS IN HIS SLEEP.

BLESS!

GROWING UP, NIALL HAD AN IMAGINARY FRIEND CALLED 'MICHAEL'!

BEFORE HARRY CAME UP WITH THE NAME **ONE DIRECTION,** NIALL SUGGESTED THE BAND BE CALLED **NIALL AND THE POTATOES!**

NIALL IS
LEFT-HANDED,
THOUGH HE USES
HIS RIGHT HAND
TO EAT AND
PLAY GUITAR!
HANDY!

'MY **ACCENT** ALWAYS WORKS ON GIRLS. THEY LIKE IT, I HAVE NO IDEA WHY.'

IF NIALL
WASN'T IN
A WORLD-
FAMOUS
BOY BAND
HE THINKS
HE'D BE A
DENTIST!
SAY 'AAAH'!

'I'M AN **EMOTIONAL GUY,** SO I DON'T HAVE TO WORRY ABOUT A GIRL TRYING TO GET ME TO OPEN UP.'

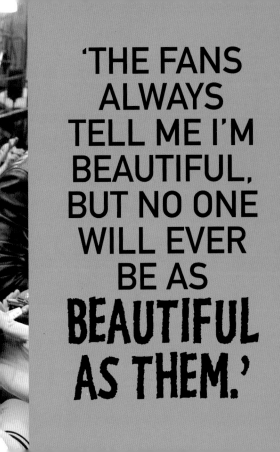

'THE FANS ALWAYS TELL ME I'M BEAUTIFUL, BUT NO ONE WILL EVER BE AS **BEAUTIFUL AS THEM.**'

'FRANKLY, I DON'T CARE WHAT OTHERS SAY.'

MUSICAL NIALL'S BEST-EVER CHRISTMAS PRESENT WAS HIS **GUITAR.**

WHEN NIALL GETS
HOMESICK THE
REST OF THE BOYS
SPEAK TO HIM IN
AN IRISH ACCENT.

'INTELLIGENCE IS SEXY.'

'LIVE LIFE
AND DON'T
SKIP TO
THE END.'